SPARKPLUG

VALVE

PISTON

COOLING
FAN

CAMSHAFT

CRANKSHAFT

D1177617

Series 601

This book tells the story of the motor car from the first clumsy steam and petrol-driven road vehicles to the modern, speedy, comfortable and mass-produced models.

Included in the magnificent illustrations by Robert Ayton are such well-loved cars as the early Rolls-Royce 'Silver Ghost', the bull-nosed Morris, the first Austin-Seven, an early Bentley, Malcolm Campbell's 'Bluebird' and John Cobb's 'Railton Special'.

This is a book for every boy—and many fathers too!

The story of the
MOTOR CAR

by David Carey

with illustrations by
Robert Ayton

Publishers: Wills & Hepworth Ltd., Loughborough

First published 1962   ©   *Printed in England*

The Story Begins

Although the motor car has now become a part of our everyday lives, few people seem to know much about its very early beginnings. For these we have to go back beyond the invention of the petrol engine in 1885 and look at an earlier form of power—steam.

As long ago as 1619, two Englishmen took out a patent covering "drawing carts without horses", but it was a French army engineer, Joseph Cugnot, who built the first truly self-propelled vehicle one-hundred-and-fifty years later. This was a heavy three-wheeled machine designed specially for pulling big guns. Luck was against the inventor because his vehicle turned over on only its second test run and no more was ever heard of it. Cugnot built another steam vehicle a year later and this second machine can still be seen in the Science Museum in London.

During the next thirty years many people tried to make a successful steam vehicle. In America a man named Evans was granted a patent for "a self-propelled carriage", his invention being a mixture of steam wagon and flat-bottomed boat. British inventors were also busy at this time, names such as William Murdoch and Richard Trevithick becoming well-known in connection with steam power.

End of Cugnot's steam wagon

Trouble in Britain

By the 1830's, the steam vehicle had made really great advances and some passenger-carrying services were being run. One man, Sir Goldsworth Gurney, began by producing a vehicle with mechanical legs instead of wheels, but he soon changed to the more normal method. His coaches at one time ran a regular service between Gloucester and Cheltenham. Walter Hancock was another inventor whose steam coaches were quite successful.

At about this time, in Britain, steam road vehicles were becoming unpopular with people who ran the horse-drawn stage coaches, and with the railway companies. Too many of their passengers began travelling in the road steamers. In fact, the opposition was so strong that in 1865 Parliament passed the Locomotive Act which imposed speed limits on the road steamer of 2 miles per hour in towns and 4 miles per hour in the country. Worse still, by the same Act, no steamer was allowed on the roads unless it had a man walking in front of it carrying a red flag. He had to be at least sixty yards ahead.

No road vehicle could possibly operate successfully under these conditions, and the poor road steamer, on which so much time and effort had been spent, gradually ceased to be used.

A passenger-carrying steam coach

From Steam to Petrol

On the Continent, where no action was taken against the steam vehicle, it continued in operation for some years. Actually, in 1902, a steam car held the world road speed record of 75 miles per hour. However, in 1885 a new invention, the petrol engine, was first used instead of steam to propel a road vehicle. The inventor was a German named Carl Benz. A year later Gottlieb Daimler, another German, made a car driven by a motor of his own design. These two men share the credit for an invention which was to change the transport habits of the world, for their efforts laid the foundation of the great motor industry as we know it to-day.

The Daimler engine soon became a great success and by 1890 it was being built in large numbers. The advantage of this engine over all previous designs was its lightness. With light moving parts and simple operation it was capable of speeds up to 1,000 revolutions per minute, whereas all earlier engines were heavy and clumsy, needing big vehicles to carry them. They could only operate at speeds of about 200 r.p.m.

Other countries began to show an interest in Daimler's engine which was soon also being made in France and, later, in America.

First petrol-driven vehicle

THE FIRST PETROL DRIVEN
MOTOR VEHICLE.
1885

New Developments from France

The next stage in the development of the motor car, as we may now call it, was carried out in France where two Frenchmen, Panhard and Levassor, began making the Daimler engine. By 1891 they had begun to produce their own cars. Daimler continued with his own designs and replaced his original single-cylinder engine by a twin-cylinder, V-type unit. In the new engine, the gas in the cylinder was 'exploded' by a glowing platinum tube which one can say was the very earliest form of sparking plug.

Another important change in car design took place around this period. Daimler and all the other car builders of the day used to mount the engine in the middle of the vehicle, underneath the seat, but Panhard and Levassor had the idea of putting it at the front of the car under a 'bonnet'. As we well know, this position has remained the most popular one right up to the present day, although some makers, particularly on the Continent, favour a position at the back of the car.

The petrol engine next found its way to America where it was used by Charles Duryea, who built a motor carriage in 1892, and by Elwood Haynes, who followed in 1894.

Under-seat engined Benz and front engined Panhard

The First Road Race

On the Continent and in America the real possibilities of the motor car were just beginning to be realised, and many of the basic design features which are still in general use to-day, were being thought of. For instance, the invention of differential gears in the back axle occurred about this time. When a car is driven round a bend, the 'offside' wheel has to travel further than the 'nearside' one; just as on a roundabout at a fair, the outside horses travel further than those nearest the centre. Differential gears allow this difference of wheel travel to take place.

By 1895, ten years after the building of the first Benz car, many well-known makes had been produced, including Benz, Daimler, Panhard and Peugeot on the Continent. In America a Mr. Henry Ford was trying, not very successfully, to build his own machine. Towards the end of that year so much improvement had taken place in motor car design that a road race was run between Paris and Bordeaux in France. The race was won by a Panhard-Levassor car which covered the 732 miles in forty-eight hours, at an average speed of about 15 m.p.h. Not very fast perhaps, but what wonderful reliability for those early models.

The Red Flag Disappears

What was Britain doing during all these exciting happenings elsewhere? She was still struggling under the handicap of the Locomotive Act of 1865. This, you will remember, made it necessary for a man with a red flag to walk in front of any mechanically-propelled vehicle on the road. This Act was really put in force to restrict the road steamer, but it applied just the same to a petrol-driven motor car.

By 1895, however, there was so much indignation throughout the country towards an Act which had held up the proper development of British road vehicles for thirty years, that it was finally abolished. From November 14th, 1896, the motor car was freed and the man with the red flag was seen no more. There was great rejoicing all over the motoring world at this news, and to celebrate the great occasion a motor rally was held from London to Brighton. Many famous motorists took part. Gottlieb Daimler was there, and there were cars from France, America and Britain, although the British cars were powered by continental engines.

The London to Brighton rally for 'old crocks,' as they now are, is still held every year to commemorate this important day in the history of the motor car.

London to Brighton run—still held every year

British Progress at Last

The year 1896, then, can be said to be the real beginning of motoring in Britain. Freedom from the red flag gave the necessary encouragement to British engineers to go ahead with their own designs.

Thus it was that F. W. Lanchester, who was a designer of gas engines, formed a company in Birmingham to build motor cars. The Humber Cycle Company of Coventry turned to car making, and the Daimler Company was founded, also in Coventry. We can see that right from the beginning, the British Motor Industry was centred in the Coventry and Birmingham areas of the Midlands where, of course, the greater part of it is to-day.

Herbert Austin, who in 1900 was working in the Wolseley Sheep Shearing Machine Company in Birmingham, made a motor tricycle. This turned out to be the first Wolseley vehicle ever made, and Austin drove it with much success in the Automobile Club's 1,000 mile Trial that same year.

Another historic event occurred in 1900, William Morris, who had been apprenticed to an Oxford cycle maker, started his own garage and built a motor cycle from parts he bought.

Herbert Austin drives the first Wolseley

Ford Struggles to Success

At about the same time that Austin and Morris were building their first motor machines, in America Henry Ford was becoming interested in making cars. In 1899 he started the Detroit Automobile Company, but good fortune did not favour him and he left. The Company itself continued, and later became the Cadillac Automobile Company.

Ford had another try, and in 1901 he formed the Henry Ford Company, but again he failed. Not to be beaten, he made a third attempt. This time he was more fortunate, and in 1903 he founded the Fordmobile Company. After only three years he was planning a production programme of 10,000 cars a year. An amazing achievement in so short a time.

The most famous of all Ford cars was the Model T, sometimes unkindly known as the "Tin Lizzie". It was first introduced in 1908. Production was concentrated on this one model because it was in such great demand. More than fifteen million were made before it gave way to new models in 1923. In 1909 a Model T Ford won the Transcontinental Trial over a distance of 4,000 miles.

It was Henry Ford who first tried to make a car cheap enough for ordinary people to buy and the Model T sold for only 950 dollars (about £240).

A famous Ford—the model T

Rapid Expansion

The motor industry grew very rapidly in these early years. In 1902 there were 209 car makers; a year later there were 300, half of them American. By 1906 the number had risen to about 700. Several more countries started making their own models, including Australia, Canada, Denmark, Hungary, Russia and Sweden. Reliability and speeds were increasing and engines were becoming more powerful. This is clearly shown in comparing two motor races. The Paris to Bordeaux race of 1895 was won by a 4 h.p. car at an average speed of 15 m.p.h. Eight years later a 70 h.p. car won a race of 340 miles at an average speed of 65 m.p.h.

Britain's first racing car was a 40 h.p. Napier, built in 1902 by a London firm of gunsmiths. This car competed on the Continent, winning the Gordon Bennett Cup of 1902 and beating a number of Continental drivers and cars.

A speed limit of 12 m.p.h. was still in force, so fast road races on British roads were not possible. But a year after the Napier's win, a special race track was opened in Surrey. Brooklands, as it was called, was later to be the scene of many exciting battles between the racing cars of the world.

Napier wins Gordon Bennett Cup race

The Rolls-Royce Partnership

Probably the most renowned name in the history of motoring was first heard in 1907, but three years before this date Henry Royce was making small 10 h.p. cars. Right from the very beginning he set himself a very high standard of workmanship, because he wanted his cars to be the best that it was possible to make. The Honourable C. S. Rolls, who was in the Motor Agent's business, heard about the Royce cars and was so impressed by them that he agreed to sell all that Royce could build.

And so it was that in 1907 the first Rolls-Royce car was produced. It was a 48 h.p. " Silver Ghost", much bigger than Royce's earlier models. Royce's high standard of workmanship was there and is still continued to this day in cars that are universally accepted as the best in the world. The Rolls and Royce partnership unfortunately did not last very long. Rolls, who was a keen sportsman, had become interested in aeroplanes and in 1910 he was tragically killed in a flying accident.

The Company continued to build cars under the sole direction of Royce. In 1911 a Rolls-Royce "Silver Ghost" was driven from London to Edinburgh in top gear only and averaged a petrol consumption of 24 m.p.g. A surprising achievement over such a long distance.

World War I. 1914-1918

Henry Ford, always a man to try new processes, introduced the idea of mass production into his factory in 1913. He realised that the only way to keep down prices was to produce his cars in large quantities on moving assembly tracks. Instead of a worker having to go and fetch the various parts to be assembled, they came to him so that he was able to work with much less effort. This is the basis of modern car building, although now a far greater number of processes are carried out automatically.

With the outbreak of the 1914-1918 war, the motor industries of the countries taking part turned to making warlike supplies. The motor car went to war too, as staff cars, transport vehicles and, later in 1916, in the form of a great armoured land ship that was to become known as 'the Tank'. Although no-one could really describe the Tank as a motor car, it was driven by a very large motor car type of engine, and was certainly a mechanically-propelled vehicle. It was invented by a British army officer.

Generally, during these four years, the motor industry contented itself with helping to win the war, and little actual progress was made with the design of the motor car itself.

British Tank in action

Birth of the Baby Car

The years immediately after the 1914-1918 war saw many changes in motor car design. Oil and acetylene lamps gave way to electricity for car lighting and starting. Tyres were greatly improved and became less liable to puncture.   But these were lean years, full of difficulties for the motor trade.   There was a great amount of unemployment in Britain and people could not afford to buy cars.

However, the car makers continued to struggle along, and in 1922 Sir Herbert Austin designed and built the very first Austin Seven.   This little car changed the whole idea of motoring.   It was the world's first practical four-seater 'baby' car, and it brought the pleasures of motoring to many thousands of people who could not buy a larger, more expensive model.

At first, people used to laugh at this tiny machine. Drivers of big cars used to complain of a 'fly on the windscreen' when they saw an Austin Seven on the road in front!   And one man said he would buy two, one for each foot!   But those who scoffed soon became serious when they realised what a good, reliable and economical car it was.   Before long many Austin Sevens could be seen on the roads.

Changes in the Motor Industry

With the arrival of the Austin Seven, many of the existing three-wheeled machines and small continental cars disappeared because people realised that the new British model was much better in every way.

Other changes were also taking place about this time. Mass-production was being used more and more in building cars. Many of the small firms which were unable to adopt this method found that competition from the cars mass-produced in greater numbers was too great, and they began to fade from the scene. Other firms were taken over by more wealthy companies to form groups. Such names as Calcott, Clyno, Bean and Swift disappeared during this period, while Hillman was bought up by Humber, later to form part of the Rootes Group of Companies.

One of the names which continued to prosper at this time was Morris. William Morris, like his great rival Herbert Austin, introduced mass-production methods of assembly, and soon his cars were to be seen in ever increasing numbers. One of the most popular cars being produced in the early 1920's was the bull-nose Morris, so called because of the rounded shape of the radiator. The same frontal design was used on the first M.G. car built by Clive Kimber from Morris parts in 1923.

The well-loved bull-nose Morris

The Fabulous Bentleys

While mass-production was being used for building the popular makes of cars, sports cars were largely still built by hand. The 1920's were wonderful years for the sports car. Brooklands track saw many exciting events, and on the Continent road races, such as the French Le Mans, were drawing great crowds, as they still do to-day.

In 1921, W. O. Bentley, an aircraft-engine designer of the first World War, produced his first sports cars. These took second, fourth and fifth places in the Isle of Man T.T. races of 1922. In the same year a Bentley won a race at Brooklands at a speed of 90 m.p.h. However, the Bentley's greatest successes were at Le Mans where it won the gruelling 24 hours race no less than five times—in 1924, 1927, 1928, 1929 and 1930. In so doing, it gave Britain a fine name in the racing world.

The 1927 win came after one of the most exciting events in motor racing history. The Bentley team was involved in a bad crash with several other cars and only one of them could be got going again. Although the chassis was badly damaged and the axle pushed back, this car was bravely driven on and finally won the race.

A Bentley leads at Le Mans

In Search of Greater Comfort

From the earliest days of motoring the majority of cars were open. The very first ones had no covering at all for driver or passengers, but gradually hoods were fitted and the Tourer came into being. Some closed cars, like the Town Carriages, were made, but these were expensive and usually chauffeur-driven. Closed bodywork was also very heavy, because unless it was solidly constructed it would shake itself to pieces.

But people were now demanding more comfort and protection from the weather, so the manufacturers started to look for lighter materials with which to build saloon bodies. One of the solutions was the use of fabric, specially treated and stretched across a wooden framework. This was all very well until an accident occurred, when it was very difficult to repair the torn material. All the same, a great many fabric saloons were to be seen on the roads.

In 1928 the British Ford Company opened its new factory on the river Thames at Dagenham in Essex, and started mass-producing cars in a very big way. Before then the Company had been assembling American-designed cars like the Model T and later types. Now British-designed Fords were rolling off the assembly lines.

Trouble on a fabric saloon body

Advances in Speed and Design

Car design underwent many changes during the 1930's. With the introduction of pressed steel bodies, the rather square box-like vehicles gradually gave way to more smoothly rounded contours. Radiators disappeared behind chromium-plated grilles, mudguards became more a part of the body, spare wheels were more neatly tucked away and closed-in luggage space was provided at the back of the cars. The Saloon Car and not the Tourer became the fashion.

Advances on the mechanical side kept pace with body changes; reliability and performance greatly improved. The ordinary family car could maintain a good average speed over long distances, while quite small racing cars were able to travel at 200 m.p.h. or more at Brooklands, Donnington Park, and other race tracks.

Most exciting of all were the achievements in the sphere of record-breaking. In 1922 the world land speed record was held by K. Lee Guinness at 133.75 m.p.h.; in 1925 Malcolm Campbell raised it to 150.87 m.p.h. First to reach 200 m.p.h. was Seagrave in 1927; 300 m.p.h. was achieved by Malcolm Campbell in 1935, and George Eyston again raised the record to 357.5 m.p.h. in 1938.

Malcolm Campbell with his 300 m.p.h. "Bluebird"

World War II. 1939-1945

By the end of the 1930's there were over two million cars on the roads of Britain. Small cars could be bought for just over £100, and for as little as £20 when four or five years old and still in good condition. Unfortunately, with the great increase in numbers, traffic problems became difficult, roads began to be crowded and accidents increased at an alarming rate.

But in September 1939 the second World War broke out and the motor industry once again turned from peace-time production to the making of war supplies. Petrol rationing restricted road travel for civilians, and plans for road improvements were put on one side. The motor car went to war as tanks, scout cars, staff cars and many forms of motorised transport.

Soon an entirely new type of vehicle appeared on our roads—the Jeep. This remarkable little vehicle was made by the Willys Company of America. It came over with the United States Army and was later in use with nearly all the allied forces. It had four-wheel drive as well as drive to the two rear wheels only. This enabled it to go over rough ground and across fields where ordinary staff cars and other vehicles could never have travelled.

The "Jeep" of World War II

Post War Difficulties

During those six difficult years of war, the motor industry had played its full part in the all-out war effort. Now it had to change back to the products of peace. It was a trying period. The right materials were scarce and car-hungry motorists had to wait as long as four years between placing an order and receiving the car of their choice. We even reached the stage when a two-year-old second-hand car was sold for more than a new one!

Petrol rationing was still in force during the early post-war years. Even if one was lucky enough to have a car, there was little petrol on which to run it. In Britain this was perhaps the motorist's most difficult period since the old Red Flag days of fifty years before. But as in those bad times when the pioneers of motoring were able to get over their troubles, so in the 1940's Britain's motor industry set to work to overcome its problems. A British driver once again raised the land speed record when, in 1947, John Cobb drove his "Railton Special" at an average speed of 394.196 m.p.h. on the Salt Flats of Utah, U.S.A. He actually reached 403 m.p.h. on one of his runs.

John Cobb raises the land speed record

Cross-Country Motoring

The first models to come off the post-war production lines were very similar to those being made when the war started. In Britain, one of the first entirely new models was in the popular range—the Austin A.40— introduced in 1947. It started a new fashion for this type of car, having no separate chassis frame, the body and 'chassis' being made in one piece. Independent springing was used for each front wheel, another unusual feature for a small car at the time.

Another brand new British model emerged in 1948. This was the four-wheel drive Land-Rover, developed from the idea of the American Jeep of World War II fame. The Land-Rover was built to travel off the roads over rough ground and it became an important vehicle for the farmer. It was also very useful for feeding and rescuing livestock during heavy snowfalls in winter. It was so successful as a cross-country car that people other than farmers quickly became interested. To-day, Land-Rovers can be seen everywhere. They are working in 160 different countries of the world, pioneering new routes through deserts and jungles, and doing jobs in undeveloped lands that only a few years ago were thought to be impossible.

Land-Rover to the rescue

Racing Improves the Breed

And so we enter the modern age of motoring, the 1950's. By this time a high degree of body comfort was demanded even in the least expensive models. Attention was also centred on performance and speed. This was the age of the sports car and several well-known companies produced new models. The 'Ton' or 100 m.p.h. was the target of every enthusiastic sporting motorist.

The Brooklands race track had been out of action since the war, as had the Donnington Park road circuit. New British tracks were built, the best known being Silverstone and Goodwood. Overseas, the Le Mans 24 hour race was still held every year and many Grand Prix events took place all over the Continent and in the Americas. Car racing rapidly grew in popularity.

Car racing is not only a thrilling spectacle. It is an important way of testing and developing ideas which may later be applied to normal cars. This was true of the old days and is equally true to-day, especially as many race meetings have sports car and production car events in which everyday models can compete. Disc brakes, which were first tried out on the race track not very long ago, are now fitted as standard equipment on many models.

Massed start at Silverstone

The Small Car Age

The 1950's also saw a change in ordinary motoring fashions. The larger and medium-sized cars continued to be in great demand, but the small car began to be seen in ever increasing numbers on roads all over the world. The small car fashion is still with us to-day, for several very good reasons.

Car prices generally have greatly increased since the war because of the high cost of materials, purchase tax, and a big rise in workers' wages. In these conditions, small cars are cheaper to buy. Petrol is expensive, and the small car will travel up to 50 miles on a gallon of petrol, so it is more economical to run. With the roads, especially in towns and cities, becoming overcrowded a small car is much easier to drive and park. Although compact in overall dimensions, the modern small car has been so well designed that it will carry four people in comfort at cruising speeds of up to 60 m.p.h.

It can be seen that small cars have been produced to meet the needs of modern conditions. They provide reliable, economical and comfortable transport for a great many motorists who could not otherwise afford the pleasure of travelling through the beautiful countryside or visiting new and interesting places.

The popular Morris Minor 1000.

A New Form of Power

Nearly eighty years ago, in 1885, Carl Benz invented the petrol engine which, with improvements and development, has continued to provide the main kind of propulsion for motor cars right up to the present day. The oil engine, or diesel, is in extensive use on many types of vehicles, but for the private car petrol has reigned supreme.

It was with some excitement therefore that we learned of a new source of power for motor vehicles when, in 1950, the Rover Company announced the world's first gas turbine car. This firm had been concerned with the development of jet engines for aircraft during the war. In 1945 it decided to continue experimenting with jet propulsion, but for cars instead of aircraft.

This first gas turbine car, which can now be seen in the Science Museum in London, was a Rover '75' with open body adapted to take the new form of power. In 1953 it was driven at a speed of 151 m.p.h. on the Jabbeke highway in Belgium and so set up the first speed record for a gas turbine engined car.

Several companies are now working on gas turbine car engines, but there are still difficulties to be overcome before a really practical engine can be produced.

World's first gas turbine car

Companies, Corporations and Groups

Again looking back to the early years of motoring we find enthusiastic pioneers building their cars in small sheds or workshops. Some had to give up and their names are forgotten. Others won fame and fortune. Yet others were bought up by the more successful companies and were able to carry on within a group.

The grouping tendency started quite early when in 1908 the Oldsmobile Company became a division of General Motors of America. In fact, in America to-day almost the whole of the motor industry is operated by a few vast groups. In Britain, although we are still lucky enough to have several healthy individual companies, the greatest part of our motor car production comes from combined, or grouped companies. For instance, the British Motor Corporation includes Austin, Morris, Wolseley, M.G. and Riley. The Rootes Group contains Humber, Hillman, Sunbeam and Singer. Vauxhall is a part of the American General Motors, while the sports cars, Lagonda and Aston Martin are operated by the David Brown organisation. A recent combining operation occurred in 1960 when Daimler cars were taken over by the Jaguar Company.

While many famous old names in motoring can only be found in the pages of history, others like those we have mentioned live on in their new family circles.

The Story Continues

The story of the motor car will go on. The gas turbine age will come, possibly even the atomic power age. It may be that in years ahead the petrol engine will be as out of date as steam is to-day. In the meantime, the car is amazingly comfortable, speedy, silent and reliable, and it can be produced at prices varying from just over £500 to as much as £8,000. It has become so much a part of our everyday lives that we cannot imagine a world without it. We use it for shopping, for business, for weekends and holidays. Father can spend a pleasant hour or two washing and polishing it, while the family dog loves nothing better than a drive into the country.

But the motor car brings new problems. It crowds our towns and cities until we can hardly move; its exhaust fumes fill the air. In the hands of careless or impatient drivers it is a menace, killing and injuring thousands of people every year. However, in spite of everything, it is a great blessing. And sometimes when travelling happily along the road we might spare a thought for those farsighted pioneers who, by their efforts, made the wonderful story of the motor car come true.

Opposite ends of motoring—Mini Minor and Rolls-Royce

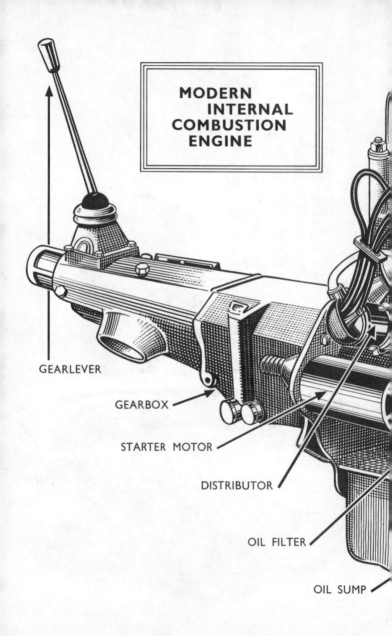

MODERN INTERNAL COMBUSTION ENGINE

GEARLEVER

GEARBOX

STARTER MOTOR

DISTRIBUTOR

OIL FILTER

OIL SUMP